CW00553571

Ten Years Flying the F-105

by

Randolph Reynolds

All photos come from the collections of Randolph Reynolds or D. Larry Patterson.

Table of Contents

I always wanted to fly and be a fighter pilot! Me at age 15 at a CAP Encampment at Maxwell AFB AL.

Preface

This book is about this young man who loved to fly and after several years was flying the F-105. There are two Parts to this story. The first is a synopsis of my early years as a fighter pilot. I started off at Nellis AFB in Las Vegas and a year later found myself going to three places in a two year period. First was Yokota Japan to join the 35th Tactical Fighter Squadron, then I began sitting on nuclear alert in Korea. In between being "home" in Japan and sitting alert in Osan Korea I was flying combat missions out of Takhli Tailand. I touch but briefly on these because there are so many men who flew combat missions during Rolling Thunder that their stories are numerous and available elsewhere.   Japan was exotic, Korea boring, and Thailand intense.

Part II of this vignette covers that period about seven years later when I am flying with the Air Force Reserve. It was wonderful to be back flying the F-105 and this part of the story reveals what our mission was and how we operated.

All in all it is a story about a man and his flying machine.

Part I

My early years as a fighter pilot at Nellis AFB in Las Vegas, the 35th TFS at Yokota Japan, sitting on nuclear alert in Osan Korea, and flying combat Rolling Thunder missions out of Takhli Tailand.

Life Begins on the Rampart Range

In the spring of 1960, I nearly flunked out of the Air Force Academy. It is not far off the mark to say that I was not well prepared for the rigors of higher education. I had been told when I first sought out a Congressional nomination for the new United States Air Force Academy, that probably I would not be academically qualified on my first try. My decision to go to the new Air Force Academy came in 1956. I wrote to Congressman Kenneth Roberts of Calhoun County Alabama, where I lived, stating that when I graduated from Anniston High School in 1959 I would seek an appointment to that Academy. One day in October of that year as I recall, I had returned from delivering papers on my paper route when I received a call from my mother. She worked as a legal secretary in town. She told me to expect my father to get me for a meeting with Congressman Roberts. Although I had started taking flying lessons the year before, my father seemed uninterested in my career goals.

I remember that meeting. Congressman Roberts, short in stature, had a very commanding presence. He had been injured in 1951 when Puerto Rican gunmen shot up the House of Representatives, killing one man and nearly killing Roberts. The congressman told me that I should work on doing well in school and to keep him informed over the next two years, and he would consider me when the time came. One of the things that I think helped convince him to support me was my long book review of Alexander P. De Serversky's book, *Airpower: Key to Survival*, a copy of which I sent to the congressman the following year. When the fall of 1958 came around, I met once more with him and he told me that if I passed my Air Force Officer Qualifying Tests, the flight physical, and met the minimum on my SATs, he would nominate me as his principal appointee. I did all that and got the nomination. There were only four other candidates in his district and I think I was the most qualified, although I certainly wasn't fully prepared for USAFA.

In May 1960 I survived a "turnout" exam in English Composition. The way we learned about turnout exams was over the PA system. I was on the freshman tennis team, at practice when the announcement came. At that moment I was somewhat inattentive to my tennis, since I was afraid that I might have flunked either math or chemistry. When the loudspeaker, located in the cadet area above the courts, announced the names of the cadets who had flunked English, I thought I heard my name. Fortunately, I had failed English because of the "content" of my final exam essay.

Of the five members of the Class of 1963 who had flunked English that spring, I was the only one to make it to graduation. In spite of the rigors of my fist year (Doolie Year) I really began to learn how much work it was going to take to survive academics. I had to take each semester one at a time in order to continue to be a member of the Air Force Cadet Wing gathered in a remote location (at the time) under the Rampart Range of the eastern Colorado Rockies. I was in very bad shape in math and physics during my second year, but because of the rigid structure and rules of the Academy, and my own burning desire, I pulled two failing grades up to passing with Cs. The following year, my Second Class or Junior year, I began to show great improvement academically. On June 5th, 1963, I graduated. The Dean of Academics, Brig. General Robert F. McDermott (who was principally responsible for the upgrade of the military academy academic programs) said to me as I received my diploma: "Randy, you made it in spite of everything we did." I survived and survived well.

With the exception of the timing of the Vietnam "conflict," I don't think I could have entered the business of military aviation at a better time. The more than 400 of us who were to head off to Air Force pilot training were not aware of how soon we would be in a war. Aeronautics appeared to me to be on the way to becoming a booming business, and the Air Force was the place to be.

The speaker at our class graduation was President John F. Kennedy. He may have sensed that we, the Class of 1963, were molded to fit into a greater vision of the future, his vision. That day seemed to be ready made to launch us into that future.

We were the first full-size class and the fifth class to graduate. I believe that the average age of my classmates was two years less than that of the four classes preceding ours. Ours was the first graduation in the new football stadium. The four hundred ninety four of us who were present (there were three others who were commissioned later for some reason) marched on in four groups. The last group had no individual I know of who made the dean's list in any of the four years, but many had made the commandant's list for military acumen. In the last two or three rows sat those of us who had been "turned out" in one or more courses in our cadet careers. If a cadet failed a course, he was given a "turn out" examination, the equivalent of a one-shot chance to pass. Failure on that exam meant expulsion from the Academy. Having been through a turnout exam was a badge of honor among those of us in the back ranks.

My year in Air Force pilot training at a base outside of Selma Alabama went swiftly and successfully. I received the Commander's Trophy as the top graduate, and headed to Las Vegas to become a fighter pilot. Not only was that sufficient to put a young man's head in the clouds but I was to be one of the first six second lieutenants right out of pilot training to be assigned to the Air Force's newest and "hottest" fighter – bombers the F105 Thunderchief. Such events appear almost routine to any observer at the time but everything that was to come to me for the next twenty years was linked back to that fateful assignment.

Craig AFB Alabama: Winter morning. Bob Rex going solo in a T-33. Bob was lost in Southeast Asia several years later.

Gunnery Training

Flying is a subject that fills my thoughts with romance and adventure. It encompasses the thrill of the man/machine interplay and the manifestation of accomplishing skilled maneuvers. I remember the feel of my first solo in the T-33, the USAF's first jet trainer. Compared to our previous jet trainer, the T-37, it was like the difference between driving a Volkswagen and a Cadillac. The T-bird was basically a fighter, and was a delight to fly. In the early 1950s systems reliability and continuity were not high priorities. Those T-33s were old, some dating back to 1949, and their cockpits had different configurations. Yet the satisfaction of flying a "real" jet was indescribably delicious for a young man right out of college.

The F-105 assignment I got at graduation from Craig has had a long lasting influence upon me.

Those things that excite us and keep us going always continue long into our memories as if they were permanently implanted into us by some demons who wanted to see how we would react fifty years later.

Those muses which pester me about my small part in the history of the F-105 are the same aggravating, self-deprecating little pests that had me spend all my time researching and recording the details of this aircraft and its history before I arrived in Nevada.

In August of 1964, I owned a 1960 grey and red, two door Buick that I had traded a 1953 green Buick Le Sabre to get. When I arrived at Nellis Air Force Base just to the north of Las Vegas, the very first thing I did was to get my car registered. I was so happy to be in the Tactical Air Command and out of the Air Training Command that just the event of putting the registration sticker with the TAC emblem on it onto my Buick's front bumper was a signature moment. I was not yet flying a fighter, but I was assigned to a place to learn to do just that — not in the old F-100, but in the brand new F-105. From the moment I learned that I had gotten the assignment, nothing else in life seemed important to me.

From any location on the base, I was aware of the purpose of the place because all day F- 105s and F-100s would be in the break or taking off. The sound of these jets as they pitched out from echelon formation over head and rolled out on downwind over the base was music to my ears.

In those days the drive from the main gate of Nellis into Las Vegas was a long one. The ride down the old Tonopah highway through North Las Vegas onto Fremont Street and then to the Strip introduced me to a world outside the gate almost as mysterious as the one inside Nellis. The real adventure came with the jet, yet the backdrop of the casinos, lights, inexpensive meals, and shows made it a carnival treat. There was nothing near the base except one casino, I think it was called the Silver Nugget. There were no tract homes, residential areas, strip malls or shopping centers. The ground east of the runways ran to Sunrise Mountain, a lone rocky prominence whose base was the perfect spot to drop tow targets. To the immediate north of the base there was a desert and lakebeds, bounded by low jagged hills and a cement making plant. At the foot of the hills were old World War II gunnery ranges we called the Flex Ranges.

Today that has all changed. Since those days, Nellis has been engulfed by housing developments, and all that accompanies such changes.

A decade past the end of the Korean War, our tactical air force was more like the Air Force of that war than it was a decade later. Not a lot of money was put into the base.

The bachelor officer quarters (BOQ) were good for the time, but somewhat substandard to those of Strategic Air Command (SAC). SAC was the nuclear deterrent and the "serious" combat command; TAC was for the adventurous, and frankly we liked the role that TAC fighter pilots played. Nellis reflected the sense of "sacrifice" in amenities that the fighter pilot was willing to endure because his one passion was flying; everything else was of no consequence.

There were seven of us in my class. We were in the "long" course, six months to make fighter pilots out of us. We were the first group of Second Lieutenants to enter the F-105 long course right out of Undergraduate Pilot Training. For us with little Air Force flying under our belts, I think we all averaged no more than 230 flight hours; this molding process would be our transformation into the small body of deep strike pilots. Between that September and our graduation in April, we were to experience the type of flying I had anticipated since I first discovered the lore of flight – fast, powerful, and artistic.

Perhaps the word artistic may seem inappropriate for what is a skill of war, yet that is an excellent term for describing this endeavor. The artist expresses his ideas and thoughts onto a medium. The fighter pilot expresses his ideas maneuvering in the air. The motion of his aircraft he commands and the precise patterns necessary to place the jet in a position to deliver ordinance is an expression of artistic skill. The canvas is the sky.

After our first trip to the gunnery range called Dog Bone Lake – the only dry lake I know of with two gunnery ranges, one at each end – I discovered that dropping small, 25 pound practice bombs on a target in the dry lake bed floor was not easy. The sensations in the cockpit were daunting because we were hurtling ourselves at the ground at very high rates of speed and we only had a matter of seconds in which to track the target and release the bomb.

There were more variables in dive-bombing than in any sport I was familiar with. We trained at first in thirty-degree dive bombing then at low altitude skip bombing, a level maneuver in which the aircraft was only 50 feet above the target. Once the instructors had confidence we would not kill ourselves, the 4520th Combat Crew Training Squadron added strafing with the 20 mm Gatling gun and firing 2.75-inch rockets.

The first time I pointed the sleek nose of the Thunderchief at the circles cut out in the desert floor, it did not occur to me that I could be killed; instead, it occurred to me that this was nothing really new to me... except that at a precisely determined altitude and dive angle I would hit the 'pickle' button — one of the two red buttons on the control stick — and pull the nose of the Thud upwards towards the sky.

I recall on my first gunnery mission four of the six practice bombs were out of the 150 foot qualifying range. The problem for us in this phase of our training was that each time we made a bomb or gun pass we were learning at an exponential rate. There was nothing the instructor could do except comment on techniques.

I can still see the circles on the desert floor the first time I shot rockets. We had been advised in no uncertain terms to pull out before we saw these little missiles impact. That was because we had to fire them at a lower altitude than when releasing bombs. When the rocket motor burned out, the inert rocket was free to wander off on its own dynamics toward the object to which it was pointed, and the F-105 pilot who watched the dust from the impact would be too low to avoid impacting just beyond it. The little 2.75 inch rockets were very susceptible to winds and misalignment at launch. I likened it to shooting a quiver of arrows from a bow while running forwards in the middle of a strong wind.

Our class of rookies did well. Almost all of us were qualified by the end of the seventh flight; if there was one thing we didn't qualify in, it was in rockets and that was due partly to the fact that they didn't schedule enough training sorties with rockets. The combat crew training squadrons at Nellis were not required to get us qualified in all events, just enough so that we were on our way to being qualified in the F105. It was left to the operational squadrons at our next assignments to finish the job.

In early February of the New Year 1965, rumor had it that the problems in South Vietnam were escalating and that the sporadic bombing of places in North Vietnam would continue. We were told that we could go down to the Wing Headquarters and in the restricted area, read some of the message traffic being received about F-105 combat operations in Vietnam. I think most of my class took advantage of that opportunity and it began to be clear that the F-105 squadrons stationed in the Pacific were involved with bombing and strafing of real enemy targets.

Later in the month I was one of two in our class to get to fly an F-105F model to Davis Monthan AFB outside of Tucson to participate in the Arizona Days open house being put on by the base. This was a very pleasant trip. On the way down, Jim Hannam and I flew instrument missions from the back seat, but I recall we flew the front seats on the return.

Davis Monthan is referred to as DM in the Air Force community and by people living in Tucson. It was the desert storage site of all the USAF mothballed aircraft. The Air Force had moved its F-4C training squadrons there, but much later DM became the home for the A-7D "Corsair II."

Hannam and I drew the duty of being on display

with the aircraft. The DM ramp was full of people and other aircraft. One of my Air Force Academy classmates, Gene Knudsen, came by while I was on duty. He was at DM undergoing his checkout as a backseater in the F-4C. He seemed to be having a good time, but from what he described about his training I was very, very grateful that I had not ended up with that assignment. None of the new pilots in the back of the F-4 were performing duties of a pilot but that of a navigator / bombardier. I never saw him again; later he was killed on a combat mission in Vietnam.

On Sunday, I think it was Valentine's Day; I was attending to the F model we had parked next to two F-104s from George AFB. The crowds had diminished from Saturday. Suddenly the Air Police drove up and blocked off the area around the aircraft parked on my line. Two pilots were delivered to the F-104s parked next to my F-105. My Thunderchief dwarfed the dart-like F-104. I sat in my cockpit and looked down on them as they cranked engines and taxied out. I sensed that something important had happened and was told they had been ordered back to George AFB in California. Not long thereafter, we got the word that their squadron had been shipped to Vietnam. It seemed odd to me that there was such a rush about it.

When we got back to Nellis, we learned that the president had ordered the bombing of North Vietnam. About a week or two later, all of us were briefed by an Air Force Captain who had been on exchange duty with the Navy flying A-7Cs off a carrier in the Gulf of Tonkin. He was on his way back to Tactical Air Command

Headquarters in Langley, Virginia to brief the staff on how the Navy was conducting bombing missions. He had stopped by Nellis to tell us what was going on. In that briefing, he brought with him some gun camera film taken from some F105s that were based out of Da Nang in South Vietnam. The film showed clearly the bombsight in the F-105. The pilot was strafing boats in a river somewhere in North Vietnam. It came home to us that what we were learning in the desert north of Las Vegas was what was being done for real in Southeast Asia.

Shortly thereafter, we were told that the new bombing campaign over North Vietnam required that more F-105s be sent to Thailand. There seemed considerable doubt as to whether one of the F-105 training squadrons at Nellis should be deployed. There was a flurry of rumors and several of the veterans gave us briefings on what to expect if we were deployed. Here we were, not yet qualified in the aircraft or in gunnery, and we were already considered candidates for the war.

We had just begun learning air refueling, something which, although not daunting, required proficiency before we flew several thousand miles over water. This commotion caused me some unease and talk of deploying ran orthogonal to my expectations. Clearly a few of our IPs were very eager to go. If what we believed had any credibility, just one squadron of F-105s hitting targets in North Vietnam would end the war in a month. Some experienced hands actually said they wanted to get over there before the opportunity ended.

It all turned out to be much ado about nothing; no

one was sent from Nellis. In the midst of this entire historic rumbling, our class received orders. I had originally requested that my next assignment be Germany. There were two wings of F-105s in Germany pulling nuclear alert and two wings in the west Pacific one in Okinawa and one in Japan. I really didn't want to go to either of the oriental locations. The assignments came down to us and had been made by alphabetical order. Allen, Hack, and Hannam were assigned to different squadrons in Germany. Miller (who at this time had slipped back to the class behind us until he could be put back on flight status by the medics at Brooks AFB), O'Donohue, and I were assigned to Yokota AB, Japan. Tate and Strabinger were assigned to McConnell AFB, Kansas, and Seymour - Johnson AFB, North Carolina, respectively.

I met a number of great pilots at Nellis. It was there we got to know Hestle, Brooks, Thorsness, and others. Hestle was shot down over North Vietnam about three years later and never returned. Thorsness became a Weasel (Iron Hand anti-SAM) mission pilot with a MiG to his credit; he also was shot down over Vietnam and became a POW and received the Congressional Medal of Honor. Brooks eventually made General, but I never connected with him after Nellis. I seem to recall that Hestle's call sign was Horse, and so whenever we flew with him we were Horse 2, 3 or 4. I liked him quite a bit because he treated us with respect, gave us encouragement, and seemed to understand that we were quite capable of becoming good fighter pilots.

My assignment was to the 35th Tactical Fighter Squadron in Yokota, Japan. I was to arrive not earlier than

30 June 1965. That was an appalling delay to me, as we were to graduate in the middle of April and I would be not flying for two months. I requested that the date be changed, and it was moved up so that my port date for departure to Japan became May 4th. Coincidentally this was the same port date as Dennis O'Donohue.

When we finished at Nellis it seemed to me that a special time in my life had ended. Little was I to know that Nellis flying would be the most fun I would have in the cockpit for a number of years. There we had only one responsibility, and that was to put all our energies into flying and learning to be a fighter pilot. It was now time to start payback for everything the Air Force had spent on my education and training. Japan, Thailand and Korea were to be my new residences for the next two years.

Some of my Nellis mates wanted to change assignments with me because we all knew that my future squadron was deployed to the war. Even if such a change were possible, I was no longer interested in a change. There is both an attraction and repulsion about going to war. I knew that this could be good for me – as long as I could stay proficient in the aircraft. That was my only worry, that as a fledgling F-105 pilot, I needed to keep flying to keep my confidence up. To this day I retain happy memories of Nellis and the excitement of those months flying over Nevada.

The new office.

Early Photo of me at Nellis AFB.

Dart Kill!

F-105s joining up just north of Nellis: Fall '64.

F-105 F formation takeoff out of Nellis AFB.
Practice Nuke bomb delivery mission.

At the RSU (Runway Supervisory Unit).

Me and Australia's Girl of the Year.

Yokota, Japan

This issue of remaining proficient in the Thud was not just a minor incontinence. For the low time pilot it was important to keep flying. A layoff of a week or two was not devastating but it created the feeling of starting over again.

Note that before the name Thud –originally a derogatory term emanating from somewhere in the F-100 world—it was referred to as the Nickel, the fifth of the century Series fighters of the 1950s.

Our arrival at Yokota on that rainy night in early May 1965 was marked by a mishap. A two seat F-105F had crashed into Atsugi Naval Base further south in Honshu. We didn't know it at the time but the aircraft had hit a railroad underpass just off the north end of Yokota's runway shearing off the main landing gear. The pilot flew the aircraft eastward towards the Pacific and both of them ejected. Unfortunately he engaged the autopilot thinking the jet would crash in the ocean but it turned back inland.

The next morning when I managed to find my way to personnel then make it over to the 35th Squadron building there wasn't much talk about it. The one member of the flight I was assigned to that was to be my sponsor met me but he was leaving shortly to go down to Takhli. He seemed eager to be going because he'd get to do a lot more flying. Before the day was out I had been temporarily reassigned to the 80th Tac Fighter Squadron until the 35th returned from its three-month duty in Thailand. They were in the process of relieving the 36th. The old 8th Fighter Wing had moved to George AFB in California and the three F-105 squadrons that were once at Itazuke Japan were now at Yokota under a provisional wing designation the 6441st.

All this was so new to me. I was in a strange foreign country, most of my squadron was not around, and I was a brand new fighter pilot wondering what sort of program they would set up for me. The answer to the latter was, hang around ops and especially the scheduling desk. Sometimes you had to make it known you needed to fly.

Yokota was a large old base. On the west side of the runway were the fighter squadrons and that included a squadron of F-102s whose defensive mission was being eliminated. On the other side of the base were reconnaissance aircraft like the RC-135, RB-47 and one RB-57. The base looked like it was some kind of industrial plant and had that feel about it. The weather that summer was muggy and often overcast. We did a lot of instrument flying and rarely got to land VFR from an overhead.

At Osan we had 24 F-105s on Nuclear Alert and kept three or four of 105s on lower alert status available for proficiency flying. If my memory serves me 24 Thuds were cocked for five minute response. The targets ranged from North Korea to the northwest part of the USSR to destroy airfields and ICBM. The latter were considered one-way missions. If you were not destroyed by Nukes going off from U.S. ICBMs you didn't have the fuel to recover any further than the Sea of Japan. We practiced the alert procedures all the time. Most of us found living in the Green House (our living and working area) was boring.

The reassignment to the 80th at least gave me something of a home. The base was really a Division commanded by Col Martin. Martin had some reason to fly to Takhli and I was told I would take an F and fly him down there, but as it turned out he elected to take the front seat and I flew most of it from the back. Our arrival at Takhli was not taken well but that was because the F wasn't considered a combat aircraft. Things changed for some of the F models later in the air war when the Wild Weasel III program started up.

Takhli

My impression of Takhli was first, this was where the real action was, and second it was all teakwood buildings and barracks. At that time we didn't have an officer's club but managed to make do at the end of one of the hooches. I got the tour of the place; I wasn't allowed to fly any missions because I had not finished my combat readiness checkout at Yokota. The cockeyed rules set by someone at the Wing (probably the Wing Commander) said that the newly assigned low time pilots (i.e. O'Donohue and me) had to have 50 hours of instrument weather time and be certified to sit alert at Osan Korea.

On that first visit to Takhli an older first lieutenant whose name I have forgotten, took me down to ops and briefed me on what was going on. Much of the flying was Armed Reconnaissance but there were strikes against lines of communication such as bridges, roads (including Mugia Pass), truck parks, etc. It was clear our job was to restrict the flow of enemy personnel and supplies from North Vietnam to the South. We were also fragged to hit Pathet Lao or North Vietnamese locations in northern Laos. This was referred to as Barrel Roll missions. They didn't count toward the 25 required missions.

One thing that impressed me was that there were only seven known occupied surface to air missile sites near

Hanoi. Hanoi and Haiphong were off limits as were targets within a fifty mile radius of Hanoi. Only the Joint Chiefs of Staff could order such strikes. We called them JCS missions. More probably the President approved those decisions. As of that date June 1965, there had been no strikes against SA-2 sites. We were not allowed to bomb any of the North Vietnamese air bases.

Back To Yokota

Well that was it for my introduction to Thailand. Upon returning home (Japan) there were more routine matters. By routine I mean getting as much flight time as I could when the 35th began to transition back and the 80th replaced them. We went to the gunnery range when the weather permitted otherwise we practice bombed on a tiny rocky island off the coast. The real news for the few bachelors that were around was that in August the dependent school teachers would be back.

Picture about four of us in orange day glow flight suits, standing outside the entrance to the Yokota officers club for lunch when Dean Rusk's party arrived in a bus filled with hibachi pots and other Japanese paraphernalia to go onboard the aircraft to take them to the states (CONUS). I was just watching when I learned about the school teachers. I had met a Japanese/Thai girl in a local bar but outside of that the bachelor life was mostly nil. When the school teachers arrived on station at Johnson AB north of Yokota that is where I started hanging out.

In the meantime the 80th arrived at Takhli in time for the first SAM targets. Besides the 80th there were two other squadrons TDY from Seymour Johnson AB in North Carolina. We were about to escalate the air war.

The F-105 And Rolling Thunder

The term "Thud" was a contraction of the F-105's official nickname, the Thunderchief. F-100 pilots (specifically who or where I do not know) had come to deride our monstrous jet by saying that the sound the F-105 makes is "thud" when it falls on the target. One bar version of the origins of "Thud" described what we did in our long legged aircraft was taxi over the target and raise the landing gear.

A typical flash back that fits into this chronology begins with one early pre-dawn briefing at Takhli Thailand when the air was cool but heavily laden with moisture. The briefing room was in a teak wood building that sat in the middle of a cluster of single story, Second World War-style buildings at Takhli. Along with about twelve other pilots I sat through the mission brief with our target displayed on a large map at the rear of the stage. We usually knew where we were going before the mission brief. This day it was deep into the populated regions of North Vietnam, a place designated as Route Package 6A or Pak 6A. If the target was within a ring of 50 miles from Hanoi or 30 miles from Haiphong, it had been directed by the Joint Chiefs of Staff (JCS) therefore referred to as a JCS approved mission and this indicated a tough mission.

There were many JCS missions, and all were within

the "restricted" areas around Hanoi or Haiphong. These areas were saturated with anti-aircraft weapons from small arms (referred to on the charts as AW) to large caliber, radar-controlled 37, 57, 85 and even 100 millimeter anti-aircraft guns (referred to on the charts as AAA). The map included numerous surface-to-air missile sites (referred to on the charts as SAM). Usually, we knew the evening before the mission what general target area our flight was to have in the morning. If the coordinates were 20 degrees north and somewhere around 104 degrees east, we knew it was a deep penetration of North Vietnam. If the latitude was around 21 degrees north, we would be in Route Package Six. That area, called the Red River Valley, was in the middle of a very highly defended area. That morning, our FRAG had ordered a deep strike to the North. The morning was not atypical, but for some reason I remember the conversation that was going on while we waited for our release from Saigon and 7th Air Force. There were more than four flights of four F-105s assigned to this particular target with nearly the same time on target.

When the general brief was over, we went into the individual flight briefs where the flight lead gave specific instructions for conducting the mission. The 355th Wing Commander at Takhli during that time was Colonel Robert Scott (not the Scott who wrote "God is My Co-Pilot"). He and his Vice Commander, Colonel Jack Broughton, established the rules for the three fighter squadrons on the field.

Flight leads were picked on the basis of rank. In the only other F-105 Wing in Thailand, the 388th at Korat AB to the east of us about half an hour's flight, flight leads were picked on the basis of experience in combat; hence a friend of mine, a newly promoted captain, got an Air Force Cross for leading a big strike "downtown" that consisted of 60 F-105s from both Takhli and Korat. I don't remember who was leading us that day, nor what our call sign was. In the first year of Rolling Thunder, the 355th Tactical Fighter Wing used automobile makes as call signs and the 388th used various types of trees. I don't remember when all that ended and the call signs started being issued with the FRAG from Saigon. Such simple and sensible call signs like Caddy, Buick, Chevy or Ford flight (which identified the base from which we flew) got all jumbled up via the computer.

Within the flights, each pilot flew in one of four positions: lead, wingman, deputy lead or number 3, and the deputy's wingman. In the stress of battle, pilot first names came into use only to get the guy's attention and to prevent confusion. I think I was Rambler 4 that morning. Regardless of what my call sign was, I was number four. I had been a first lieutenant for two years and never led more than an element. The major who was leading us had about the same number of missions as I had. He was on a PCS tour from Seymour Johnson AFB back in North Carolina. That means he was transferred to Takhli on a permanent relocation (over six months) and he had previously been flying F-105s in North Carolina.

At that time there were only three bases in the United States that had a combat group of F-105s. In addition, there were two bases in Europe (Germany) and two in the Pacific (Japan and Okinawa) that had F-105s. I was on temporary assignment from Yokota, Japan. I made four trips to Takhli, ranging from one month to three months' duration, between June 1965 and December 1966 to fly combat missions. I was considered "temporary help," as were a number of other pilots from Japan and Okinawa.

The three lieutenants on my flight sat around the briefing area for a while. The word was that we were on hold for weather. Generally speaking, just after the flight brief we would be deep into our own thoughts. It took about twenty minutes to "suit up," that is put on our g-suit, flak vest, parachute and helmet and "step" to the bread truck, which would deliver us to our jet. This particular morning, at 0330, it was still pitch dark and we were sitting around for almost an hour.

One of the topics of conversation was superstition. We all had our little superstitions. Who wouldn't? In the four months I had spent at Takhli on rotation, we averaged someone shot down at least once per week. Usually the losses came in bunches depending upon the intensity of the raids. There were only so many Thuds left then, about 600 of 830 F-105s built, but by the end of Rolling Thunder I think there were less than 200 F-105s left. One report gave the figure that we had lost 372 D models. There were only so many qualified pilots in the pipeline to replace those who finished up their 100 missions over the north.

So it appeared there was a finite end to our (Thud-drivers) participation in the war. The name of the game was to survive 100 missions and go home alive with this combat tour on your record, a few medals, and a future in some other kind of flying.

Two of the superstitions we had at the time were,

"never have your photograph published in the press," or its corollary: "avoid interviews." The genesis of those superstitions may have come from the experience of Lt. Col. Robbie Risner. Col. Risner's picture was on the cover of *Time Magazine* one week, then not long after that, he got shot down and captured. His story is well documented. Risner was the squadron commander of the 67th TFS, "Gamecocks" which was an F-105 unit based at Kadena Air Base in Okinawa. His "enthusiasm" may have contributed to his squadron having experienced the worst loss rate of any F-105 unit in the war to that date.

Another superstition was the hanging of tiger teeth from a necklace worn underneath the flight suit. The Thais said that tiger teeth were good luck charms, and many of the jocks purchased them. I, for one, kept a small key chain given to me by a girlfriend I had met at Johnson Air Base (Iruma Air Station) in Japan. It had the Katakana symbol for good luck on it. I kept that talisman in the left sleeve pocket of my flight suit. I am not superstitious, but there is something vaguely reassuring about a "thing" that you take with you to link you to a more sane world beyond the war.

Years later, when I was a commander leading F-105 or F-4 flights on long missions somewhere, I carried a small silver cross that my then future wife had given me. I had met her at the halfway mark in my two-year tour in Japan. Her name Vonna Thompson might be a clue to her Norwegian ancestry. She was just starting her second year as an elementary music teacher for the dependent school at

Johnson Air Base north of Yokota when we met at the Officer's Club — but that is a fairy tale story of its own to be recorded elsewhere.

On this particular morning, when the word came down to launch, our thoughts became very focused to the task at hand. I was flying with the 357th Squadron, but the aircraft to which we were assigned might have been some of those that my squadron from Japan had left there the previous November when we had been ordered to leave our aircraft for the newly assigned permanent squadrons.

The change in priorities from nuclear deterrence in Korea to Rolling Thunder in Vietnam had taken place. After December 1965, I didn't know the maintenance crews as well as I had when they were assigned to our squadron from Yokota. The previous fall we had deployed as a squadron, and we knew all our crew chiefs. Out of a sense of trust and respect for their work some of us would skip the pre-flight of our Thud and just check the bomb fuse settings prior to climbing into the cockpit. This day, however, I followed the checklist.

The air war had begun with the idea that this effort was temporary and the local fighter squadrons in the Pacific Theater would be assigned to the work. A year after this mission the US was continuing to pour more men and aircraft into Thailand.

The reason we had been put on hold that morning was inclement weather in the target area. When we were released, we were still fragged for Tai Nguyen rail yards. Tai Nguyen was in that most heavily defended area northwest of Hanoi. Just after we came off the tankers, we heard the lead strike flight call that it was switching to the target frequency and that they were inbound down Thud Ridge.

The mission lead reported a solid undercast as far as they could see, and recommended that the mission hit alternate targets. This was not atypical. The rail yards came up on the schedule again about two days later, and the aircraft scheduled for that opportunity were loaded with two of the new QRC-160 jamming pods, which were supposed to foil the Fan Song (SA-2) radars.

This time the mission succeeded, and due to the significance of the target coupled with the first use of the pods, the strike lead was recommended for the Silver Star, and I believe that all the participants were put in for Distinguished Flying Crosses. (I should note that up until this time, the temporary squadrons at Takhli either didn't make the effort or didn't consider such missions worthy of combat awards and decorations. With the arrival of the permanent squadrons at Takhli in the late fall of 1965, officers were assigned to write up awards as often as possible.

The rail yards and the steel mill at Tai Nguyen were first hit that spring, and were targeted many more times later in the air war. The QRC-160 pods worked, but because of the shortage of pods only the aircraft on JCS missions to Pak Six would carry them, and for a while only the flight and element leads were fragged for them. This meant that the elements had to work in concert to ensure the pods remained effective, as the North Vietnamese were adept at adjusting to our new tactics.

The experience of "strapping on" a Thud was always a pleasure for me. I can imagine a hundred years before, a young cavalry officer getting into the saddle for a charge into the fray. Perhaps he would have felt the same about his horse and his confidence in riding into battle as I did about my jet. I loved the Thud and came to know its every nuance. The only thing I hated was the possibility that something would break or go wrong after I had gotten started, and I would have to rush to a spare aircraft, if there was one. If we were already out of the chocks, there would usually be a spare aircraft with a pilot listening on the radio. The option when someone aborted either before or just after takeoff was to launch the spare pilot. Any aborting pilot might feel a certain amount of angst about the man who went in his place with the spare. The spare pilot sitting on the ramp was either scheduled to fly later in the day or already had one mission earlier in the morning and this would cause him double jeopardy.

The usual reason for an abort was if the crew chief at the last chance inspection found a hydraulic leak or cut tire. On my third tour, I was aborted in the arming area twice, and once, as number four, was forced to abort because the aircraft in front of me aborted and popped his drag chute in my face after I released brakes. I wanted to taxi back and take off, but the maintenance rules were such that they had to inspect my tires and brakes before I could take off again, and I never would have caught up with the flight. After three straight aborts, the squadron commander came to me and told me not to become impatient because I might take an airplane that really was in bad shape. He was correct in reminding me of that.

Sitting in the cockpit of the 105 I did not feel as if I were in the largest jet fighter of the day, but it was true. The cockpit was expansive compared to the Thud's predecessors; one could get seriously hurt if he jumped from the cockpit to the ground.

The normal procedure for starting the Thud on the ramp at Takhli was to use the black powder cartridge that was inserted into a duct leading to the starter motor underneath the front part of the J-75 engine. The idea was to see if we would all start simultaneously. There was no requirement to be that precise on our start time but it was fun to see if we could make it happen just on the tic of the second hand of our issued watches. All that was necessary was to depress the red cart start button on the left console and that would ignite the cartridge sending black smoke billowing out from the underside of the aircraft and starting the rotation of the motor. The acrid smell and rushing sound could be sensed even as high up as we were. At eight percent of the engine rotation (8% RPM) we would move the large throttle from cut off into the idle position. Usually the engine would light off and begin to run before the RPM got to 20%.

If the cart didn't fire the crew had to wait five minutes then remove the cart and start the engine with the ground power unit. This would result in the pilot having to rush his pre-taxi checklist – but something we learned to do by skipping some of the steps until later.

On this day everything worked as it should and soon I was aware of the vibrations and sounds from my jet as it woke to life. I usually taxied with a set of earplugs in my ears under my earphones that were mounted inside my helmet. I have sensitive ears and I knew if I didn't protect them my hearing would be damaged. I have always hated loud noise.

With the canopy open, my helmet on, the heat of Thailand caused sweat to pour down my face. I had to taxi with my oxygen mask dangling loose just to keep the perspiration from clogging the valve. It always seemed hot there no matter what time of year it was.

With six 750 pound bombs strapped to a rack on the fuselage centerline of the jet the aircraft had a tendency to sway from side to side. We didn't taxi fast nor did we rush the turns. When I lined up on the runway we either formed up in an echelon fashion or in a sort of fingertip with the number 4 man in the slot behind the space between lead and two. This resulted in a lot of turbulence rocking the jet in the slot and I often would reduce my power to reduce the temperatures on the engine while I sat back there in the jet exhaust.

From my vantage point of being at the back of the formation I could see the concrete stretch of runway disappearing toward trees some mile and a half away. I was supposed to watch the exhaust plume from the jets in front of me for the change in color as water was injected into the engine to drive up the thrust in afterburner by another 2000 lbs. We needed every ounce of push we could get from the J-75 and if the water injection failed the pilot was supposed to abort.

An early abort was not a problem but once the F-105 was up to nose wheel rotation, about 155 knots, it was too late to stop in the runway we had remaining. If the color of the exhaust turned from a blue green to orange yellow the water was making it into the hot section of the engine. If not I would call "no water" over the radio and let the Thud driver ahead of me make his own decision.

This morning when the number 3 jet released his brakes I hit the button starting the second hand on the clock. As the second hand hit eight seconds I moved the throttle outboard with a flick of my wrist and dropped my feet down releasing the brakes. The big jet began to roll and since I had timed it right the exhaust nozzles opened when I came off the brakes and within two or three seconds the afterburner lit thus I gained a few more feet on the runway in max power.

On a hot day with a heavy load the pressure of the additional 6000 lbs of thrust felt in the cockpit was a lot less noticeable than on a cold day in Korea with no bombs. I checked the oil pressure and EGT then simultaneously flipped the switch to turn on the water injection. I knew it was working by the green light behind the small square indicator that read "water inj" and the very slight increase in forward thrust.

My next point of concentration was to look for the 1000-foot marker on the side of the runway and then look at the standby airspeed indicator to see it jump off the peg and begin reading. At 2000 feet I needed at least 105 knots on such a day to tell me that I was accelerating properly. As the Thud accelerated there would be a low but clear squeal on the headset from the antiskid generators on the wheels.

When my jet reached 150 knots I knew that there would be a bit of a delay in acceleration as the ram recovery took hold, and between 155 and 160 knots on the tapes I brought the nose up with a positive motion of back pressure. The feel of the stick in the Thud seemed directly linked to the rate of rotation of the nose, a control characteristic that made flying the airplane a joy.

The airplane felt like it wanted to fly and it would get airborne about 175 knots. From that point on to about 200 knots I was in a sort of dead man zone if the engine quit as the jet was too low or too slow to safely eject, later this was still the case with rocket boosted ejection seats installed.

After a rapid gear retraction I reached for the flap handle at 200 plus knots on the calibrated airspeed tape. When the flaps were up the jet would move quickly towards 250 knots and I started a smooth but relatively steep turn to the left to cut off the other flight members for our join up. It was about then that I noticed the water injection light was out and I came out of afterburner and left the throttle full forward accelerating to as high above 300 knots as I could get before I was established on the inside of the flight leads turn. If I played everything just right I could be joining up in lose formation on number 3 before he began to tighten up his turn and reduce power to slide inside the leader.

At this time I was oblivious of the early morning haze and the low sun beginning to break over the eastern horizon. As soon as I could I moved the pressurization lever forward to pressurize the cockpit and this would often bring condensation in the form of what looked like smoke into the cockpit. We had to put the pressurization lever into ram or off in order to have the water injection function. I usually used the manual setting to get cold air because the automatic setting was slow at responding.

As I joined on number 3 I slipped low enough to make sure all his bombs were still set on the racks and that there were no fluids pouring from the aircraft. Then with me hanging on his wing we would slide in on the leader and head east-northeast. Takeoff and join up that day were precise and satisfactory. Now we would hope for a successful mission into North Vietnam to add to our counter.

Going North

There was a significant threat facing those of us flying Thuds in Rolling Thunder, more so than in any air combat situation since that time. Some pilots who had experienced Korea said it was worse than what they faced in Korea; certainly after two years of attacks on North Vietnam their air defenses were formidable and capable of adjusting to our change in tactics.

I do not think it was possible for any of us doing the bombing to feel strong emotions about the North Vietnamese as an enemy, but they could and did frighten us with their anti-aircraft fire. They were knocking us down and this made us determined to hit back. There were times when it registered on me that beneath the flashes and rising pillars of dark grey cloud from my or my leader's bombs in that moment were people we had killed.

It was a high adrenalin activity; no other that I know of could match it for intensity. I believe that had the North Vietnamese threatened my home or posed a lethal threat to our survival as a nation I would have been more positively motivated towards the war. As it was the flying was the best. We were very good at what we did as fighter pilots and this was satisfying. If we finished a combat tour it would be a good thing for our careers and that was good.

There were some of us who believed we could win

the thing (the war) given a free hand but that was not a view expressed by anyone in any of the fighter squadrons I flew with. We were there as McNamara indicated, to control the situation not to destroy Vietnam as a nation. Typically the sense we had of our work, the shooting back, was that as bombers our job was to deliver the bombs on the target assigned and get out of the area as fast as possible. What happened on rare occasions was that some jocks would get to shoot at enemy aircraft and this was the quintessential motivation of the fighter pilot. One against one and most of us felt quite able to win in such a fight.

An example of how this altered the mind set of those of us dragging the heavy cast iron bombs up north is reflected in a mission I was part of to hit a railroad bridge on the northeast railroad not too far from Hanoi. This mission took place in November 1966 and I remember it more clearly than any. The target was not far from Kep, one of the more active North Vietnamese airfields. The flight I was in was assigned to be flak suppression, that is we were carrying CBU-24s, a recently development cluster bomb dispenser. The cluster bomb would open up just above the target and release hundreds of small bomblets when impacting would obliterate personnel, trucks, and guns.

The plan was for us to be the lead flight into the target area. I don't recall any other flight assigned flak suppression. Our target would be the antiaircraft guns located, according to the photographs, south of the railroad bridge. The remaining strike aircraft. I think there were three flights of four Thuds on that mission with us beside the Iron Hand (Wild Weasel) flight that was going to be in the area, would bomb the bridge and the railroad. We could expect heavy flak and perhaps some MiG activity. If the day was clear the latter would certainly be about and the SAMs (SA-2s) might not be too active.

It was a long flight up to the coast to a point north of Haiphong. I remember that the clear skies helped ease my tension, I was number 2 in the flight. It was one of the clearest days I'd ever seen over the North and that meant that navigation would be easier and we could see SAM launches from a long way away.

We cruised in at a "medium" altitude about 5000 feet above the ground at 420 knots ground speed, until we got on strike frequency and then we dropped down to about 2000 thousand feet above the ground. We would hit the range of the known SA-2s just before we got to the target area for we had planned the route to edge along the 25 miles radius of their range till the last moment when we would have to penetrate that airspace. Everyone knew that once we were setting up from the initial point (IP) through the popup maneuver to the bomb release we could do nothing about dodging any SAM that rose up toward us.

We pushed up to only 480 knots leaving us power to go faster if we needed. The flight leader had me positioned on the right wing because he planned on being slightly north of the guns and would roll in to the south. I was positioned slightly down his wing line out about 2000 feet when he started his pull up maneuver. I remember that there was very little chatter on the radio at first.

The strike aircraft were lagging a bit and we were the first in. Suddenly my lead transmitted that he was rolling into the right and he began a hard roll across my nose. Since I was scanning between him and the ground for the target this took me by surprise so I pulled up hard and rolled left then right to get spacing on him. In so doing I was working the controls rapidly and at the low speed, I slowed to almost 300 knots, too slow for maneuvering a Thud, and I caught a glimpse of the caution light coming on. It was a large amber light on the right side of the instrument panel.

I had two thoughts, *they are starting to shoot* (I could see the orange tracer rounds sailing up toward me) and *my gosh something's wrong with the airplane*.

I allowed myself a quick glance at my hydraulic gages and they were bouncing about from low to high pressure. I realized that I was, in my anxiety, manhandling the controls, I eased off my control inputs, let the nose of the Thud slice down and the caution lights went out. By that time I could see my leader pulling off and so I tracked the spot on the ground beyond him for my release point.

At first I was unsure if I had the gun emplacements located then I saw his CBU's sparkle as they impacted and so I shifted my roll in slightly to the right of his impact.

I steadied the aircraft and let the sight track up.

When everything looked good I hit the pickle button on the stick and felt the bombs release.

I kept the nose down for a split second, rolled hard right, unloaded a bit then pulled hard left and up. This was to foul up anyone who was tracking me.

I looked up to see where my lead was but I didn't see him at first.

I then rolled back right to look over my wing and saw

this massive area of smoke on the ground, probably two or three times the size of a football field and I knew we had all hit in the target area.

I saw no more tracers and I felt good.

I looked again for lead and then our number three called and asked where he was. He called and said he was climbing slowly to the north of the target area heading northeast.

Since I was lower I looked up and in the distance I picked the silhouette of his aircraft against the sky.

At that moment as I began to join up we heard a call that there were MiGs in the area. Immediately I began looking and rolling hoping to clear myself.

Then came another call from one of the other Thud flights saying that two MiG21s had passed between them and another flight headed north.

Our flight lead said he would turn north and join in the chase.

Immediately I got excited. I reset my sight for air-to-air gunnery and turned on the air-to-air radar just in case the opportunity came.

In those days this took about four movements of various switches, the radar mode button was changed, the radar turned on, the sight setting moved to caged or air to air, the weapons select knob moved to gun, and since it was automatic for me to turn off the master armament switch once I left the target area I turned that back on. (Later they modified the F-105 so that one switch would change the mode from bombs to air gunnery (MiG-Killer mod).)

I was in a very loose formation off lead and three and four were trailing us about a mile.

The flight leader who had called the MiG sighting reported that he was still headed north. I think all of us were now engaged in the hunt.

The worst of the mission was over and we had, at least my flight, succeeded in hitting the target and clearing the way for the others. Now we might get a chance to engage the infamous Mig-21.

This didn't last long.

In a matter of minutes a loud, overpowering transmission from one of the surveillance aircraft off the coast blasted our eardrums with the code for warning that aircraft were approaching the buffer zone on the Chinese Border. I don't remember the exact words after all these years but it could have been similar to: "This is Red Crown, Warning, Warning, Aircraft entering the buffer zone exit to the south, exit to the south, coordinates Yankee Foxtrot, Yankee Foxtrot!"

There was a twenty nautical mile zone away from the Chinese border that we were to stay out of and a ten-mile zone from the border that if we penetrated we might be subject to a Court martial.

Well the MiGs had obviously flown into China to shake this pack of mad Thud drivers. We all turned back towards the coast and checked our fuel. I was in good shape fuel-wise although we were all below the target area bingo. I figured if I couldn't refuel, no tanker around or something wrong with my systems, I would climb to 30,000 feet over the Gulf of Tonkin and coast down to Da Nang. As it turned out our number four man was really low on gas something that was not unusual as the number four man often ended up having to play more with the throttle to stay in formation than the rest of us.

The KC-135 tanker was just where it was supposed to be when we got off the coast nearing South Vietnam and lead let number four tank first. I was, as always, after such adventures quite hyper and feeling much relieved. It wasn't until then that I really appreciated the work of the Iron Hand flight; the NVA must have been reluctant to launch SA-2s in our vicinity for fear of retaliation from the Weasel and his escorts.

The return to Takhli was routine and we looked good in formation on the last stretch.

When I entered the debriefing shack there was the bottle of Wild Turkey — which we were allowed one shot of if we wanted. I sat and talked to the Intel officer about the details of what I saw. When I was finished someone asked me if I would be willing to be interviewed by the Stars and Stripes Newspaper. I was so hyper I agreed to it in an instant.

What I didn't know was that in a couple of days a tape of that interview and a press release had hit my hometown. It was the first my parents had ever heard about my flying combat missions. I had never told them that even though I was "stationed" in Japan I was spending about a third of my time flying missions out of Thailand.

Since on each of my trips to Takhli my orders were for a 60 to 90 day TDY tour I needed to get as many missions called "counters" as I could during these rotations. Yet it was not crucial because I fully expected I'd have to finish a full tour eventually even if I was rotated back to the states for a while.

Counters were those missions that were credited toward the100. Missions over

Laos didn't count and they were referred to as LBJ missions. We logged counters as "O-1.2" in the flight log; LBJ missions were "O-1.37."

When Rolling Thunder began all that was necessary to complete a tour was 25 missions over North Vietnam. That was rescinded almost as soon as it was announced and the total was raised to 50. We thought that based on the number of "counters" each squadron pilot was getting in the summer and early fall of 1965 this was an inordinately high number. When the required missions to complete a tour rose to 100 we said, "There ain't no way!"

From the fall of 1965 through the winter of 1966, no one had completed a tour. In time, we learned what our predecessors in Korea and the latter stages of World War II learned – there is a way to survive. The first two Thud drivers to finish 100 missions from Takhli reached that number in April 1966. We thought of them as celebrities, but the Air Force just looked at them as returning assets from a short overseas tour. Because they were on permanent change of station orders and had finished in less than six months (regardless of the fact that they had been on temporary duty to the Pacific Air Forces, referred to as PACAF, the year before), they were permanently relocated within PACAF to finish their tours. That was not what they wanted.

I never found out how many F-105 pilots finished 100 missions between 1966 and October1968, when a broken

President Johnson halted the bombing of North Vietnam. There were a lot who wore the 100 mission patch after the war. Some Thud pilots volunteered for second tours. My personal knowledge is of only two that succeeded in completing a full two hundred missions over North Vietnam in the Thud.

After 63 missions and two years in the Pacific Theater, I was shipped back to the states to become an instructor pilot. I volunteered to return to combat in F-105s after six months as an instructor pilot in the T-38 but the "rules" prevented that course of action. The ramp up of pilots into the war had by then depleted the ranks of instructor pilots available to the training command and I was told I had to be on station for two years.

When I had reached the number two spot for re-assignment on the volunteer list for a second combat tour the rules were changed. I had to remain an indefinite time on the base until a certain number of non-volunteers had been sent to Southeast Asia. My chance never came and I always regretted not having completed 100 missions over North Vietnam.

Two combat configurations: Left aircraft with two 750 lb bombs (during bomb shortage), right aircraft with two 3000 lbs. bombs.

F-105s at Takhli ramp circa spring 1966.

On the tanker.

Heading North Nov '65 in a Silver Nickel.

Haulin' Baby Hueys -3,000 lb Mk-118s: fall '65.

Jockeying for position on the tanker.

Out of Takhli 1965 - 1967. 6, 750 lb bombs.

Launching for a mission up North.

Part II

Post War Thud Flying: My experiences with the Thunderstick II (T-Stick) F-105s and the very first two overseas deployment of an AFR fighter unit. This is where I got very close to all the experienced people that made the fighter business in the Air Force Reserve a success.

The F-105 Joins the Air Force Reserve

Completing a tour in Southeast Asia was harrowing for those who flew everything from fighters to O-1s. However, flying the F-105 in combat set the Thud pilots apart from many others who took up that sort of work. Today air combat like that in Vietnam is quite different. The tactics, aircraft, and electronics have completely been transformed from what was, although a lot faster, essentially World War II type flying.

In 1972 the Air Force began turning the remaining F-105s over to lucky Air National Guard and Air Force Reserve Units. The Guard units had been in the fighter business all along, but the Reserve units had been flying old C-124 Globemasters, so they had quite a transition to make going from trash haulers to fighters. Since these would be the first fighter aircraft in the Reserves since the 1950s there was some angst within the AFRES Central Command about losing what we referred to as "trash haulers". When the change came about none of the old AFRES pilots were put into the F-105. The transition from four engine C-124 prop aircraft (Korean War Vintage) to single seat fighters was difficult but eventually it worked.

I left the Air Force in 1970 to get an advanced degree. When I heard about the Reserves getting fighters I jumped at the chance to fly F-105s again.

Proud to be back flying F-105s at the 301st TFW/457 TFW.

457 TFS circa 1979.

I gave the wing Director of Logistics Col. John Collier a range ride upon his retirement.

Willie straps me in.

My crew chief Willie Hedges and I share an after mission brew.

Flight of 4 over Lake Worth just north of Carswell.

T-Stick

Humpbacked T-Stick F-105 on 301st ramp.

To appreciate the capabilities of T-Stick F-105s one must understand what Tactical Air Command was trying to accomplish in the later stages of Rolling Thunder. During the bad weather months in North Vietnam we were often precluded from hitting targets. The Navy had overcome this problem with the A-6 attack aircraft. The A-6 had a pilot sitting next to a weapons systems officer, both of which were able to fly in weather and at night using their advanced navigation and bombing aides. At the time the USAF did not have that capability.

At the time General Ryan was the PACAF Commander, the Air Force tried using F-105D models with improved radars, referred to as Ryan's Raiders. It was a failure. Four of the first six aircraft so modified were lost in less than a month. The mission was eventually cancelled soon after that. However, attempts continued to modify certain D models, some of which had been severely battled damaged (080 twice), by installing Loran C navigation systems and an internal navigation system known as GAVRS (Gyro Attitude Velocity Reference Set). This was a trick since the D model's weapons control and navigation tube-type systems dated from the mid-1950s and the Loran system was difficult to integrate with those older systems. All this equipment was mounted along the backbone of the aircraft under what became to be known as "The Hump". The Hump was also good for storing extra drag chutes on TDYs — much better than using the gun drum, which pissed off the gun plumbers when a forgotten chute trashed the gun drum during a range mission.

After modifying 30 D models, the active duty could not maintain the T-Stick systems, much less ever get them to function as designed. TAC gave up on the idea and turned all 30 over to the 457 TFS in the 301st TFW newly established at Carswell AFB Texas in Fort Worth. After a lot of hard work, the 301st CAMs avionics troops got the T-Stick stuff working as advertised and continued to maintain it in good working order. In the spring of 1974 I joined that squadron and in time became the full time Air Reserve Technician (ART) Quality Control / chief FCF Pilot. A dream come true!

The 301st TFW had three fighter squadrons. The 457th

at Carswell, 507th at Tinker and 508th at Hill. All the pilots had a lot of serious combat experience, most in the Thud.

It is worth noting that the F-105 was designed to fly five thousand hours yet on many of those jets we had exceeded that number. The tragedy that really brought this to attention was an F-105 that lost a wing during a training mission flying with the Kansas ANG at McConnell AFB. The accident board found that stress corrosion cracks in the forward and aft wing attach lugs were the culprit. We started out having a field team inspect these lugs with magnetic rubber every 150 flight hours later those flight hours were increased but the work load was stupendous. Initially none of the aircraft ever had the wings pulled and getting the pins out that held the wing in place on the lugs was a very difficult and tedious job. If a crack were found that could not be ground out to the acceptable limits the F-105 was "struck" a Navy term for permanently grounded. We were fortunate in the 301st at Carswell as none were out of limits and most had no cracks. (These hairline cracks were too small to see directly.) The opportunity it gave me was to test fly a lot of F-105s for engine changes, stabulator actuator changes, and wing pull inspections and the like. We averaged one a week for five years and I flew most of them.

One other problem was the rudder stabilization system that was part of the aircraft's automatic stability and control design. The stab aug, as we called it, could be turned off in flight but the jet was more sensitive to flight control inputs and could lead to over control. The problem was pervasive in that we had numerous pilot complaints about getting spurious inputs to the flight controls. Not a good thing when flying at 100 feet above the ground. The climax came when an aircraft I was scheduled to fly, but was given to another pilot, did an abrupt wing over and crashed from 3000 feet above the ground. I was number four in that fight and witnessed what happened.

The recent history of this aircraft, tail number 513 was that I had grounded it on a test hop the week before for many anomalies. Those were supposedly cleared and this was the scenario. One of the pilots in the squadron, Bob Woodard was to lead a low level strike flight to the gunnery range and his wingman would be flight examiner or check pilot. Carl Decker was his name and maintenance sent down the list of tail numbers for this flight and Woodard got 513. I had them switch it so I would fly 513 so I could see if the discrepancies were worked out. Car Decker had 161 that had been having problems with its nav system so on the way out of the ops building, I mentioned to Decker that since he had 161 he might end up with a heading problem. He suggested that we swap jets so he wouldn't have to worry about the heading thing. I told him that I had FCFed 513 the week before and had a bunch of write-ups on it. That didn't bother him so we swapped. The result was disastrous for Carl.

After we started the mishap investigation on 513, I was convinced that somehow, even though the stab-aug system had been cleared, it had contributed to Carl's crash. However, we never could prove that. It occurred to me that perhaps I should have FCF'd it one more time. One never knows. That was the business in those days. The wonderful thing was that every time I asked anything of the technicians in maintenance they did their best to complete the job to my satisfaction. Eventually the avionics shop techs demonstrated that if two wires short in the stab aug system causing a link to ground a hard over in the rudder would occur and that would have caused 513 to go into an abrupt rudder roll.

The next three chapters are about deployments that we made with the Thunderstick II F-105s, affectingly referred to as humpbacks, since all the Loran gear was put inside a modification on the upper fuselage that looked like a D model with a big hump.

Norvenich, Germany 1977

Coronet Poker was the 301 TFS deployment to Norvenich, Germany in Aug 1977. Of all the deployments to Europe we had, this—the first overseas AFR fighter deployment—remains in my memory as clear as if it were yesterday. I suppose it is because of the initial glitches we had and the continual crummy weather we experienced throughout the deployment. Also, I am constantly reminded of it, and in my garage hangs the complete map of our redeployment across the Atlantic. Somewhere in my files I even have the original flight plans.

All of us in the 301st FW remember our first wing commander Brig Gen. (eventually MG) John E. Taylor—a WW 2 & Korean War veteran who had flown P-51s, F-84s (bent and straight wing), F-86s, F-100s, and now the Thud—as having that "can do" attitude, and consequentially expecting that we in the 301st could always do better with less. Although General John had been around and done many things, I think he had a blind spot when it came to how much he could expect one person to do.

Deployment

My job was to be on the advance party to Seymour Johnson—the base in eastern North Carolina from which we left for Germany. Not only was I to be on the launch crew for the jets out of SJ, but I was to be in charge of the launch. That meant I had to be there before the Thuds and maintenance crews arrived. The plan was, once we got them launched, I'd join the maintenance party on board the C-141 and get over to Germany on the last flight in.

I deemed it necessary that I be in Seymour *more* than the 48 hours General Taylor thought necessary in advance of the launch day. Our active duty Air Force advisor Col. Ralph Budde (all advisors were lovingly referred to as a RAFSOBs — Regular Air Force Son Of A Bitches) was to go with me and act as the senior representative for the wing.

Budde was on his retirement assignment, and I had been with him on trips before. His interest lay in having a good time and avoiding any real work. Early on the morning three days before the CAMS (Consolidated Aircraft Maintenance Squadron) was due to arrive at SJ, Budde and I hopped into F-Model 261 and headed off for North Carolina. I was in the back. (Colonels get priority.)

That flight over to SJ raised the hair on the back of my neck. It was a stretch to get to SJ from Carswell on one hop, but Budde figured we had enough fuel, so not to sweat it. I ran my own flight card (Form 21) and concluded that without any delay and a staying at altitude — above 24,000 — until we were nearly there we would be on final with 1,500 pounds of gas — minimum fuel for the Thud. The problem was that we couldn't take any deviations or we would find ourselves running tight on gas.

Those of us who had a lot of experience in the F-105 knew how to do what is today called a climbing cruise or to take advantage of the reduction in fuel weight to reduce the fuel flow. Budde didn't even bother. He set the power and left it there no matter what. His logic, I suppose, was that we would gain speed as the jet weight decreased.

Well, in the ATC environment with vectors and altitude changes, this didn't work. We had about a third of the way to go and I recalculated our expected fuel burn and told him that if we didn't ask for priority and start easing off the fuel flow we would be on final with emergency fuel.

He ignored me, or it just didn't register with him. Sure enough, had it not been for the good weather at SJ things would have been real dicey on approach. We landed with less than emergency fuel in the tanks. I suppose Taylor would say, "So, you made it and it worked out."

That started three days of aggravation for me. Budde and I checked into the Q, and then he wanted to go the club. I wanted to meet with the Chief of Maintenance at SJ (they had F-4Es as I recall) but the Colonel was in no hurry. That began three days of pure hell. Budde essentially disappeared, and I was left to coordinate the arrival and departure of the 24 F-105s that were to come in.

Despite what our Wing Mobility Officer, General Taylor, and the 301st FW Ops Officer had told me, the 4th TAC Ftg Wing was not prepared for us. They had just coordinated a dozen Weasels from George launching out of there two days before and they were not thinking of *us*.

I got six hours of sleep in the next 72, bouncing from one office to another, making sure everyone at SJ that was in charge of anything was ready for us. The precise timing of the arrival of the 301st CAMs folks I do not remember, but we made a big mistake in the way we parked the jets. It may have been a miscommunication between me and whoever was in charge of the flight line guys, but we stacked the jets as they arrived with the first scheduled to depart in front of the next eight, and the next eight, and so forth.

On the day of the launch, with the first cell cranking up, the people preflighting the jets behind them were being blown about. But, that wasn't the crisis. The crisis was to come later.

After all the Thuds were put to bed the day they arrived, the flight line folks disappeared—many went downtown to hit the ville. I had put out the word that start engines for the first cell was six A.M., or maybe that was the scheduled take off time. Whatever the case, it was right at dawn, and I wanted everyone back on the line by 0400. In the meantime, the jocks went into crew rest—of course, as always many stayed at the club for a long time.

Since Budde was having a good time with the "boys" at the bar I was the only contact person that the SJ Command Post had, so I kept getting many calls about this problem and that problem. The funny one was, I got a call very late in the day from someone who said that they wanted to know if the jet that General Taylor was flying in a D model? Well, on the frag we had given TAC it included the tail numbers. The response was of course yes it was a D (he wasn't about to fly in an F). Soon thereafter came that silly dance in which I was told to get the message to Taylor that he had to fly in 309 (an F) and would not be allowed to fly by himself. My response was to tell TAC that he was in crew rest, but that we would get the message to him later. I didn't want to tell General

John about that, so someone in Ops took the message to him.

Of course, when it was all said and done, we played the subterfuge game of having the F "broken" so he would have to fly the D spare, then maliciously "fix" the F in time for the next cell to launch with some other pilot. So, Taylor led the flight over in a D. As I said, Taylor was not about to fly a two-holer, so of course, we played the same game on the way back.

Man! The next morning I had *real* troubles. I arrived on the flight line about a half hour before the pre-flights were to start and there was not a soul from the 301st around. I was panicked. At 0400 (or whatever gosh awful time it was we were supposed to be there) only a few crew chiefs had come. We had planned to rotate crew chiefs from jet to jet since we were spread thin with maintenance people. In very short order, I had jocks showing up in the dark to jets that were not pre-flighted.

I was missing about a quarter of the crew chiefs, and we had to launch! It was going to be a disaster. We would not make the launch time, the Thuds would miss the tanker rendezvous times, and the whole thing would be busted.

What saved the moment was the weather over the Atlantic. It had turned sour and Coronet Poker was put on a 24-hour weather delay.

Thank God!

The rest of that day we helped the few active duty George AFB F-105G folks fix a couple of their broken jets. Can you believe it? They were trying to mount a *P-1* type hydraulic pump on to the *ATM* instead of the bigger utility pump! Like that was gonna work! Gosh, their maintenance was bad!

Well, we reorganized but didn't move the jets. I learned that the bunch of flight line folks that were late showing up had gone into town on a bender and had not gotten the word on when to show up. The next morning I made damn sure everything was organized much better, except the way the Thuds were parked, the jet exhaust problem was a real havoc for the last cell to launch.

When all 24 got airborne, I was *so* relieved. Even that gosh awful flight in the back of the C-141 to Norvenich was a snap. I slept most of the way. We arrived late that night in Germany.

Once settled in our quarters, the Maintenance Control Officer Capt. Larry Patterson and I shared a room with the only phone in the place. I remember crashing on the bunk only to be awakened by someone calling for Patterson. The phone would wake me up almost every fifteen minutes so I just ripped the cord out of the wall.

I think I had only gotten about three hours of sleep when someone was banging at my door telling me to get dressed and down to the operations building for the first ops area briefing. I was so groggy I just remembered the big map of central Europe, the NATO officer telling us about the no-fly zone, and that none of us could fly until we had a local area check out. Good grief!

I watched the limited flying opportunities slip by as the weather continually befuddled us. The day we sent off a flight of four who ended up in Denmark was the day even the *Germans* wouldn't fly. That's bad weather for sure!

Typical rainy, foggy day in Norvenich.

I finally got my first opportunity to fly when it was decided to put a German fighter pilot into the backseat of the F model so that a few more of us could get our "local area" check out. That day, it was VFR, which is visibility somewhere between 3 and 5 miles as long as you remained below the overcast. The low level that we were to fly was across central Germany and went over little villages and down rivers. By the third or fourth turn, I was getting lost and had to do everything on time and heading. All the hills with towns on top looked just like all the other ones. They all had orange-red tile roofs and were all packed together.

Finally, after about twenty minutes of this the German guy in the back said to me, let's knock this off and go have fun. He took the controls, and for those of you who ever got to fly in the back seat of a F model you know how limited the forward visibility is — ziltch. Even experienced Thud drivers can only get the jet down to about a mile out from the runway when flying the back seat. This guy tells me to turn off the IFF. He turns sharply to the east and says not to worry about the buffer zone and we blast into it.

After a while he turns back northwest and we go up to a British base that had Jaguars (the Brit attack fighter bomber) and we get permission to do a couple of low high speed passes right down their ramp. All this time I am wondering who gets shot after this is all over, me or the German F-104 guy.

It was quite a flight and I learned quickly that the NATO bases were very hard to see at low altitude. Norvenich was surrounded by a forest. After flying in west Texas with visibilities to the horizon, this stuff reminded me of flying low levels in Japan, except there were mountains all over there.

The weather clears enough for a two ship to finally launch.

My next flight was the FCF. I hung around while the troops changed the engine. I had seen a lot of these, but there in limited conditions, with only the stuff they brought in the WRSK — well it was a sight to behold. Too bad none of the senior brass was there to watch — especially the RAFSOBs. I learned a lot about how really good our maintenance guys were.

My only concern was how was I to get the thing flight tested if the weather was IFR all the time.

Waiting it out in the German rain.

Well I certainly didn't want to have the guy who was to fly it back across the pond to be doing a flight check on the *engine* on his way. I don't recall who was scheduled to fly it home, but I think Ops said if the weather prevented me from doing the FCF they would take it home as is. My feeling was, not on *my* watch, even if I had to break the rules I would get the jet airborne. Therefore, I did, and I was in the weather from gear up to 35,000 feet.

When I broke out, I ran out in AB for a bit, I couldn't see what was beneath me so I stayed subsonic. Then they gave me a radar vector back to Norvenich through the murk and I checked as much of the airplane as I could. Not a problem with anything. The 301st CAMs had done its usual top-notch job.

To give a sense of all this, let me say that over half of the test hops I did out of Carswell revealed some problem. I never left any system unchecked, so even though the FCF was for an engine change I'd do the full airplane check just as if it had come out of depot maintenance.

As I was climbing out, I remember thinking that if there was a problem with the gyro (The T-Stick IIs had problems with the HSI drifting off), or with the radio, or with the engine I had no alternate to fly to, and even if I did it would have been pointless since the whole country was clouded out. Therefore, I glued myself to the instruments and just went for altitude.

There is something about flying in weather; it is sort of like being in a cocoon. All is dark grey outside, sometimes its bumpy sometimes smooth but you trust that the controllers are keeping you from hitting anyone and you sense that you may be the only one in that space at that time.

When I broke out above the clouds as far as I could see was just a solid undercast. That is one of those moments you treasure, even if it's for less than a minute, there is no earth, just you and your jet, and you get the feeling that you trust each other.

The next night, the night before we left for home, most of us were "Germanized". We were at the German AF club and had to crawl through a rough board tunnel where at each turn point someone would stick their hand through a plastic sheet with schnapps and we'd have to down it before going on. At the end, we climbed up and out only to be grabbed and put into a sort of stockade where they stamped "Germanized" on our foreheads and we had to chug a beer.

I still have the bent J-79 compressor blade on the wooden stand with the German maintenance officer pin welded to it that they gave me. The F-104 maintenance was contracted to someone like BMW. Their jets were immaculate, clean, fresh paint, and I know they looked down on us for having such dirty looking jets. But of course, they learned that our old Thuds were in just as good flying shape as their shiny F104S zippers.

Long high flight

My next episode is about losing sight of everyone over the mid-Atlantic when the tanker we were with left us in the clouds. That was the longest high flight I have ever had: Norvenich to Carswell in 11 and a half hours.

We had to return 18 Thuds across the pond. The normal set up was three flights of six. We were to depart near mid-morning and due to our westward progress, we would land in Texas eleven hours later, but in the early afternoon. In contrast to launching out of Seymore Johnson at pre-dawn, this re-deployment *should have been* a piece of cake.

The U.S. Army got into the act by providing customs inspections just prior to our getting to the jets. This was all the more aggravated by the German "lunches" that had been prearranged. We would normally carry a box lunch with simple things like some cold chicken, and apple, a candy bar etc. The German mess hall way over did it. I remember getting in a line running along tables in their mess hall with a huge white plastic bag in my hand. These large women, I suppose German cooks, filled the bag with all sorts of stuff that would be great for a picnic, but were useless in the cramped conditions of the cockpit. How anyone expected us to eat this stuff I do not know. The bag was filled with mostly sandwich fixings and fruit.

By the time we got to the customs line with our parachute bag, parachute, extra water, maps, and hardhat, we were quite loaded up. We had to drag our regular bags along so that they could inspect them as well. Someone had us put the baggage on a pallet. I remember doing a slow burn when they insisted I clean the bottom of my jogging shoes!

Fortunately, it was a fair day in Germany, but by the time I got to my jet, 465, I was already behind the schedule. I was in the second flight, but I was also to get on the radio early because I was designated a spare for anyone who had trouble in the first flight.

Sure enough, I got the word just after pre-flighting and, trying to find a place to stuff my German lunch, that someone was having trouble in the first group and I should get started. As soon as I came on the radio I learned that I would move up to number 6 in the first flight that Maj. Frank Peck was leading. I caught up with them in the arming area and we were off for the states. I don't remember who had to drop back. I think the last flight had all the Tinker jets.

During that trip the European Air Traffic Controllers had gone on strike, but our tankers out of England had been given permission to meet us on the regular route. In my opinion, not having to deal with controllers, especially in Europe, was a relief although we did have to get support from the ground stations.

I don't know if it was the lingering effects from the Germanization Party that we went through, or what but I had to relieve myself before the third refueling or about three hours into the mission. In fact, I had to relieve myself often — so often that I filled up the urine bottle that was stored in the left rear console. The only other vessel that I had to piss in was a canteen full of water that I had brought along to supplement the cold water in the thermos that was mounted on right rear of the ejection seat. In short, I had to drink the canteen down in order to empty my bladder, but of course drinking all that water only made me need to go more often.

The good thing about the F-105 was that the attitude hold of the AFCS was reasonably reliable and so what I did as number 6 was to pull out from the formation about 2000 feet from the tanker, turn on altitude and heading hold, unzip the poopy suit and my flight suit then fumble around through the long underwear and get everything lined up to do this. As long as there was not a major course correction, this worked fine. I do know of fighter pilots who just gave up and let it go onto the cockpit floor — a fool hardy if not hazardous thing to do. I don't recall anyone in that flight reporting trouble; at least I had my canteen.

About halfway I took one of the go pills the Flight Surgeon gave us, I can still picture whom that was, but I have long since forgotten his name. I am sure it is on the planning documents that I have cleverly stashed in some box in my basement. So I never felt tired the whole flight. However, the boredom of flying around 24,000 feet over a dark grey sea in and out of high clouds was soon to be broken by a bad moment.

We were in a cell with three KC-135 tankers out of England. At exactly half way across the pond, we were down to one tanker to top us off, and he was to then pass us onto a single tanker coming in from the states. I believe the new tanker was an ANG guy. I think Frank Peck started asking who had Loran lockons, and 465's loran was solid. A couple of us agreed with Frank that we were off course by a couple, or three miles. The last tanker nav said he had us dead on track. Whoever was right didn't matter because *someone* was wrong. At that point, we were to pick up visual on the new tanker, but we were in and out of cirrus clouds.

Our tanker called us to say that the new tanker was at eleven o'clock for so many miles, and then he just peeled away and left us looking. All twelve eyeballs were straining the horizon looking for the tanker. At that point, none of us had enough fuel to abort to Lajes in the Azores.

In short that was the critical point over the north Atlantic in which we knew we would be low on gas, so the hand off had to go well. It didn't.

Suddenly several of us saw the new tanker to our three o'clock about three miles away pop out of the clouds. Frank pulled around into a hard left turn and made a cut off to intercept the tanker. I think he called for the tanker to reverse course. As number six, I was thrown out wide trying to catch up. Then I lost them all in the clouds. This was not good. I kept my turn up, dropped below the cloud deck and looked up to where I expected to see the flight.

No one in sight.

There was so much chatter between Frank and the KC-135 crew that when I called that I had lost sight of them no one was paying attention. I rolled out and heard the tanker pilot call that he was reversing track so I hesitated for a few seconds then started a gentle right turn. Then after what seemed an eternity I spotted — very far off — the tanker and the other five strung out behind him.

Frank was getting angry about this time and told the tanker to stay out of the clouds. He reported that he would have to start a turn in order to do that, and Frank told him to go ahead and we would make the join up.

Frank later told me, "I wasn't angry — just scared shitless!"

I was so afraid that I'd lose sight of them again that I lit the afterburner and went for them.

Frank was pulling up to the pre-contact position when I called that I was catching up. He then asked for a fuel check and I had under 4,000 lbs, which by that point made me the low man. He cleared me in to get a gulp then I moved out and we cycled in order.

It was with a great sigh of relief, better than taking a piss into a full canteen, when I got gas. There was no place to go and had I lost sight of them it might have taken a long time to rectify that situation in that weather. I suppose I was at a state of high PRF.

The rest of the journey was pleasant. We got out of the weather short of the coast and came down the east coast, picked up some tankers (these I am pretty sure were out of the Phoenix Air Guard and they were pretty snappy) near Atlanta. After we did our final top off, we were free to accelerate and climb on the last leg back to the house. I recall we did a six-ship fly by at Carswell.

Earlier in the flight, a fly appeared in the cockpit with me and he would occasionally fly around as if he were enjoying the view. I wondered at one moment how a person on the surface below us would describe the motion of that fly at 24,000 doing little circles while moving along at about 300 knots. When I opened the canopy, he flew out and the thought stuck me that he might be a virulent strain of fly and I could be accused of introducing a predator.

After all, it was a great deployment. The first thing I did after getting out of the cockpit was to dump out my canteen onto the ramp beneath the tail. Our wives met us at the jets and Vonna didn't understand what I was doing. I later threw the canteen away along with the rest of that German lunched.

Gulfport ORI 1973

One of the advantages of having a one of a kind aircraft is that no one in the active duty Air Force has a clue as to what you are capable of doing or not doing. The truth be told that the Thunderstick II F-105 was, as demonstrated earlier, just a regular F105D when it operated in the U.S.

Loran is a low frequency long range system designed for ships not high speed fighters and most Loran stations are oriented outwards from the coast over the water. However we were supposed to demonstrate its effectiveness to the RAFSOBs but of course we made things look good on our ORI. The way we passed the bombing demonstration of our first ORI was to take several Thuds to Gulfport Mississippi where it was expected that we could get Loran lockons. We'd been there before but did mostly regular air to ground gunnery on the Air National Guard's mostly secluded (home build) gunnery range in the middle of the great forested expanse that covers most of Southern Mississippi.

Our ORI was different in that we had to navigate with the Loran and drop bombs in level flight at 150 feet using the Loran and our autobomb release system. I don't think there was a pilot among us who felt that this could be done with our antiquated equipment but some wise folks figured out that if (a big if) we could get the Loran signal to work for just a short period in the flight all we had to do was "Hold" the signal to the boxes and visually flight to the target. By holding I mean we locked in the bomb release with the pickle button on the stick but leave the Master Arm Switch off.

When the target came into view we were in basically a high skip bomb mode. The weapons setting switch had been taped by the inspector so that we would not go from Loran to Manual. We didn't have to, and by using the master arm switch "release" BDU33 bomb rather close to the target.

This is not to say the Loran system couldn't do as well but the system had to be fully functioning for it to do so. Once I was successful in seeing that happen. We passed that phase of the ORI. I believe the 12th AF IG had wind of some gimmick we could do but they never mentioned it.

Gioia del Colle, Bari Italy 1979

Our next deployment was to Italy and that trip also had its foibles.

Southern Italy, especially near the heel of the boot, west from Taranto is in the low income status. There is an Italian Base there at a place called Gioia del Colle. In World War II it was a medium bomber base but in 1979 they were equipped with F104S Star Fighters. Our experience there was entirely different than in Germany. The weather was not a problem. This time it was the mission. We went there with our "sister" squadron the 507th from Tinker AFB Oklahoma. The country side is dry and flat. The vegetation as I recall is sparse and the base was not well funded.

This deployment was unique in several ways. Unknown to most who were involved—a 457th and 507th combined extravaganza—the Italians at Gioia del Colle were unhappy about our deployment.

As part of the Checkered Flag training concept, this base in the heel of Italy was to provide us with a forward operating location in case one of the many war scenarios occurred. The reason the Italians were unhappy was that USAFE had deployed a squadron of F-111s down there the year before and the Italian Air Force had not yet been reimbursed for the expenses that they incurred.

None of this was told to those of us who went on the site survey in January 1979. We had been held up at Ramstein AB in Germany for two days waiting for the weather to improve enough to fly a C-9 in and take us to Italy. (Picture snow, black ice, fog, and damp cold.)

The USAFE team that was to accompany us was not very helpful. When we came off the aircraft in Gioia del Colle we were met by two very somber Italian Air Force officers, one of them was their DO.

In January our small team from Texas came to Ramstein AFB in Germany on a "pre-arranged" planning conference. That didn't go so well. I was there to arrange for our aircraft maintenance bed down, but I was also involved with connecting with the operations people since our senior member, Colonel Dick Cotton as I recall, was tied up with the USAFE mess. When we managed to get the C-9 to Gioia the 20th Stormo Commander was not willing to allow AFRES to use the base until USAFE paid the $2 million (I am certain it was dollars and not lira) that was owed. What ops had for buildings was an operations shack on the ramp that was used to house sheep. Our maintenance was to be housed in a concrete fuel truck bunker at the far end of the field.

This site survey was an adventure in itself due to the bad weather and the fact that our military orders ran out the day we left. We were supposed to wait back in Rein Main Germany for a C-141 to haul us back to the states, but before we left for Italy I pointed out to the SATO office that our military orders were expiring and we had to leave on schedule. They booked us on a Pan Am flight back to NY.

I have since been to Italy on personal travel and fell in love with the country but on that day when we stepped down from the aircraft the reception was as cold as the weather in Germany.

This trip was marked by an incident that could have been disastrous. It involved a 507th F model that was being flown on this particular mission by someone from Tinker that I didn't know well.

Up until this point our pilots did not make a good impression on the Italians. One example was that when they came to the Club on the first Sunday in their flight suits to eat, things got testy. I think the jocks expected to use the bar; but Sunday's at an Italian Officer's club is set aside for families in their Sunday best. The 457th pilots were asked to leave, I think, by 507th CC Col. Jed McEntee. This along with the fact that we never felt welcome by the 20th Stormo kept relations on the chilly side for some time.

Two things happened that help break the ice. The first was that the Italian officers put together a very sumptuous buffet for all of us. Each of the senior members of our group gave our counterparts a gift. The gift I gave to the Chief of their Maintenance was a large wood plaque with a pewter inscription. In my presentation I mentioned that we were much more alike as a flying unit than they realized because, like us, they had to operate on a rather austere basis.

The interesting point to me was that we could be

friends (most of them spoke English) and the Commander liked my plaque so well he took it away from the Maintenance Group and kept it for himself. I had a red cloth cover that my wife made just for the plaque.

Gear Collapse

Another reason that this was an interesting deployment was that the F model that came over—one of Tinker's—had an unsafe gear indication on one mission and the right main gear collapsed on landing.

I still have one artifact from that incident. In front of me on my desk is the pin from the F model that caused the problem.

The culprit.

It is a large bolt with a special short, narrower threaded

end on it. The flange on the other end has a flat spot. That flat spot was where the upper swing brace (trunnion) hit this pin after it backed out from the over center link of the main gear linkage.

I learned that the F model gear was different from the D's. The problem that happened would not have occurred on the Ds due to the slightly different configuration. The cause was that the safety wire that was supposed to be in place on the nut end of this bolt either came out, or was not properly safety wired by Tinker's maintenance. Eventually the nut came loose and allowed the pin to slide far enough to protrude out into the plane of rotation of the upper gear strut.

That was what we learned after the jet slid off the runway. We had been fragged on this particular day, near the end of the first week on the deployment, to carry 500 pound MK82 inert bombs to some gunnery range. The flight lead was someone from Tinker I didn't know and he was going to take the F with Doc Almand, our senior Fight Surgon in the back seat.

It seemed as if all of the days were high overcast, and this day was no different. I was on the handheld radios down at the cave of a Maintenance Control Center that we had established in that old NATO fuel truck bunker when I heard that there was a problem with the gear on the F.

I drove down as quickly as I could to the control tower and hurried upstairs. Jed McEntee was the overall ops commander, as our Wing Commander Brig. Gen. Scheer had cancelled out on this trip. Jed was down near the runway.

I was listening to the radio conversations between the

lead and whoever was trying to check out his right main gear. There seemed to be some doubt as to whether or not this was just a malfunctioning warning light, or whether or not the problem was serious. The 105-1 allows pilots to land with one gear unsafe (not any two). After cycling the gear a couple of times the pilots made the decision to return to land.

Since they had inert bombs on board I was concerned, and I remember calling on the land line to Jed, or the SOF (Supervisor of Flying), whoever it was, and suggesting that if the gear appeared up, to attempt to jettison the ordnance before coming back.

If I remember correctly, if the gear uplocks were not engaged the normal arming circuit to the MER would not be energized, but they could punch off the centerline rack with the jettison button. This wasn't attempted. I was a bit concerned that if both gear collapsed on landing the centerline rack with bombs would rip up the belly of the aircraft and, like the B model that landed gear up on the MER at Hill about three years before, it would probably destroy the jet.

They made a long straight in and I could see 287 touch down. I held my breath. There was about a ten knot quartering head wind. The F rolled down about 1,000 feet past some large shed that was near the runway. When he got past the shed the right main folded. The jet started skidding on the right drop tank and the wing tip.

About 6,000 feet down and just off to the side of the runway were a fire truck and other emergency vehicles. The F slid off the runway and headed directly toward those vehicles. It came to a halt in a cloud of dust just short of them.

The front canopy opened up and the pilot hopped out, and then immediately went back to the rear canopy and started gesturing. The rear canopy was still shut. At first, I thought Almand was having trouble opening it up.

I was concerned as I watched all this through the binoculars that the aircraft might catch on fire. It didn't but there was a real sense of urgency in the Tinker jock's manner. It seemed forever before the back canopy opened and the pilot and our emergency crew got Almand out.

This incident was a major headache. Yet as it turned out the Italians were the greatest in helping us get the F back on its feet. They had a crane. They brought it over, and using shoring and mattresses to protect it, they lifted up the wing and our folks got the right main gear down and locked into place.

The Italians helped us get a tow tug and bring it back to the ramp. There was some sheet metal work that needed to be done, but overall it was in fair shape. I think one of the hydraulic reservoirs in the wheel well had a bad leak after the impact and that plumbing would need to be repaired along with a few other minor items. However, we deemed the engine was not damaged by all the dirt and stuff that was thrown up.

When I had the chance to do so, I checked the cockpit. Wow! The back seat ejection seat had been armed and Almand, in his distraught state of mind, was about to blow himself out. That was what the pilot had been gesturing about.

The configuration of the front seat revealed that the main gear handle had remained up but the emergency gear lowering handle had been pulled. This seemed odd to me but it would not have made any difference, the bolt in the joint of the right main was not going to back into place anyway.

Once the aircraft was back on the ramp, I climbed into the cockpit to see what condition it was in. I discovered that the pilot had not precisely followed the checklist. The gear handle was up; so what he did was put up lock pressure into the system, then used the emergency gear release handle. I suppose, in the thick of things that is how he read the checklist procedures. Everyone was fortunate on how this turned out. Doc Almand, however, gave everyone a scare. According to what the 507th jock told me, Almond had raised the *ejection seat handles* sometime after they had run off the runway. The pilot knew he had an armed seat and was trying to get the Doc to hold his hands away from the ejection seat. Fortunately, the battery was still good and they got the canopy open and extracted Almand. I don't think anyone disabled the seat by cutting the line from the seat trigger, but I never knew how all that was finessed.

That incident broke the communication barriers between the Italians and us. From then on, we had a good time on their base.

A maintenance crew from Tinker eventually went back over to repair the bent bird. About six weeks after we got home a 457th pilot (Capt.) Hayes Kirby) went over to fly it home to Tinker. To this day, I don't know why someone from the 507th didn't go over. Hayes had to wait in Europe for quite a while until he could join with two other Air Force jets that were headed back across the Atlantic with a tanker. Knowing Hays, he made good use of that time though.

Party with 20th STORMO 1979. Bob Jones and me on far right.

Reception Gioia del Colle 1979. Jones left, me right.

Photos of 287 by Col. Jed McEntee.

After The F-105

In the summer of 1981 it became evident that the 301st at Carswell would be equipped with the older model F-4D Pave Spike / Loran D aircraft. We had been speculating that a change had to happen because the old J-75 was becoming unreliable. There was a rumor supported from 10th AF that we would get F-111Ds since the Air Force was having trouble with that upgraded version. It seem to many that would be a disaster for a single squadron and I think the USAF thought the same for as soon as the Korean and USAFE fighter bases started receiving F-16s they were more than eager to move the Phantoms they had to the Reserves. We (301st FW) already had two squadrons of F-4s, one at Homestead AFB Florida and one just getting started with the 924th TFG at Bergstrom AFB outside of Austin Texas.

This proved to be a challenging mission for us. Operations had to find Weapon Systems Officers (WSO) for a Reserve Squadron and to transition all the single seat, single engine pilots into twin engine jets with two men in order to be combat ready. Maintenance had to "gold plate" inspect and repair each F-4 that came from Korea or Germany because they had been so neglected as the F-16s arrived there.

Solving The WSO Shortage

Since we were all used to flying solo in the aircraft, having a WSO was going to be a learning curve. The shortage of eligible back seaters was a real headache. At one point General Scheer, the 301st Wing Commander asked me to look into making the F-4 single seat by moving all the weapons and radar up to the front cockpit. Since I had once worked for MacDonald Aircraft on the F-15 I had a small "in" to that company. What I got back were sketches and descriptions of how it could be done but at the cost of a million dollars apiece. That was the end of that idea.

Bye bye Thud, Hello to the Double Ugly

The new and the old in 457th colors Note Loran "towel bar" antenna on the double-ugly.

In the early summer of 1981 the 457th received a loner F-4C and Roger Strantz and I were sent to McConnell AFB in Wichita, Kansas where, after twenty hours in the front seat, we got a similar number of hours in the back seat learning to be IPs. For a while things were fine because we were dual rated in the F-105 and the F-4.

In time the F-105s began to disappear from our ramp. My beloved 465 went to Davis Monthan AFB for storage and eventual decapitation. Some went on pedestals and others went to train ground crews in making rapid battle damage repairs. The last place Thuds operated from was the 508th FG at Hill AFB in Utah. That was the sight of two "Thud Ins" or Farwell parties for the Thud.

In time I inherited the 457th as Squadron Commander and really enjoyed that assignment. Not long after we become Combat Ready and passed our first F-4 ORI with an excellent. I got rumors that I was wanted in three units. Brig. Gen. Dean Erwin had taken over for General Sheer who went to 10th AF as CC, and ultimately became the AFRES Commander, wanted me to take over the 924 TFG in Austin. I did not feel I had enough experience for the position and would prefer to take on the Wing D.O's job that had been vacated. In no uncertain terms Erwin made it clear that if I didn't take on the 924th my advancement in the Reserves would be over. That was that. Bye by Fort Worth, hello Austin.

I had loved the F-105 and I know so many jocks who did as well. It was a great run for that Aircraft from 1956 to 1981.

About the Author

Randolph Reynolds — still a fighter pilot at heart.

Randolph Reynolds is a former jet fighter and instructor pilot for the United States Air Force having flow the F-105 Thunderchief (10) years and the F-4D Phantom (4) years. During that time he was a squadron and group commander. During this time he spent five years as the Chief of Quality Control in F-105 maintenance for the Air Force Reserve. He accumulated over 4500 flight hours. In 1988 he was hired by the National Aeronautics and Space Administration (NASA) to head up a new Operations

Engineering Branch. He continued to fly flight Research Aircraft until 1997 when the Ames Research Center Flight Directorate was closed. He was offered the job as transition head of the relocated Airborne Science operations at NASA's Dryden Flight Research center.

Reynolds retired from the Air Force Reserve with over 30 years of service in 1994 and retired from NASA in late 1999. He then spent ten years teaching courses in aerodynamics as a faculty member at the Prescott Arizona campus of Embry-Riddle Aeronautical University.

Colonel Reynolds graduated from the United States Air Force Academy in 1963 and completed his Master of Science degree from the University of Arizona. He received the Hugh L. Dryden Memorial Fellowship from NASA in 1993 and did post graduate studies in physics. He currently resides with his wife in Prescott Arizona.

Printed in Great Britain
by Amazon